Surveys

for

Conversation

By Deborah F. Hitsky

PRO LINGUA ◯ ASSOCIATES

Pro Lingua Associates, Publishers

P.O.Box 1348
Brattleboro, Vermont 05302-1348 USA
Office: 802 257 7779
Orders: 800 366 4775
Fax: 802 257 5117
www. ProLinguaAssociates.com
Email: info@ProLinguaAssociates.com
        orders@ProLinguaAssociates.com
SAN: 216-0579

*At **Pro Lingua***
our objective is to foster an approach
to learning and teaching that we call
***interplay**, the **inter**action of language*
learners and teachers with their materials,
with the language and culture,
and with each other in active, creative
*and productive **play**.*

This book was set in a variety of fonts with the idea that the surveys should be fun and varied, and that, since the pages are to be removed from the book, each should stand alone. The illustrations are selected from three collections of clip art: *Art Explosion®: 750,000 Images,* Copyright 1995-2000 by Nova Development Corporation and its licensors; *The Big Box of Art™,* Copyright 1997-2002 by Hermera Technologies Inc. and its licensors; *IMSI MasterClips®: 1,000,001 Premium Image Collection,* Copyright © 1990-2001 by IMSI. The book and cover designs are by Arthur A. Burrows with suggestions from the author. Printing and binding are by Boyd Printing of Albany, New York.

Printed in the United States of America
First Edition, First printing 2003

CONTENTS

CONTENTS

Spring   49

Summer   73

CONTENTS

For my family and my students,

who are my family, too.

LET ME INTRODUCE MYSELF

The name I'd like to be called in class is _____.

My address is _____.

My telephone number is _____.

I have _____ brothers and _____ sisters. Their ages are _____
_____.

My favorite color is _____ because _____
_____.

My favorite food is _____ because _____
_____.

My favorite free-time activity is _____ because _____
_____.

My favorite place to be is _____ because _____
_____.

The most important event in my life was when _____
_____.

These are the schools I have attended before this year:_____
_____.

I came to this country because _____
_____.

NOTES

Topic _____ Name _____ Date _____

Information, Please!

I am a <u>day/night</u> person.

My favorite pastime is _____.

I enjoy _____.

I don't like _____.

A sport I enjoy is _____.

I would like to have a _____ for a pet.

My favorite food in this country is _____.

I like reading books about _____.

I like watching television programs about _____.

Something I can do very well is _____.

If I had enough money, I would buy _____.

If I could change my life, I would _____.

What I like about living here is _____.

What I don't like about living here is _____.

NOTES

Topic _____ Name _____ Date _____

Back to School

In school this year, I want to improve my . . .

_____.

This year, I'd like to study . . .

_____.

Some class activities I enjoy doing are . . .

_____.

Something I don't want to learn or study in English class this year is . . .

_____.

If we take any field trips this year, I would like to go to . . .

_____.

A problem I have with English is . . .

_____.

The best thing I can do in English is . . .

_____.

By the end of this course, I want to be able to . . .

_____.

For me, English grammar is . . .

_____.

The adjective that best describes how I feel about the English language is _____.

NOTES

Topic _____ Name _____ Date _____

Fall Fall Fall Fall Fall

Fall in this country makes me feel _____.

What I like about fall is _____.

What I don't like about fall is _____.

When I was younger, one fall activity I enjoyed was _____.

Since moving to this country, one activity I enjoy in the fall is _____.

When I compare the fall in my native country with the fall here, I see that _____

_____.

Of all the four seasons, I like _____ best.

Of all the four seasons, I like _____ least.

Before winter begins, I would like to _____.

Fall is the best season for _____.

NOTES

Topic _____ Name _____ Date _____

My Native Country

My native country is _____ . I left it because _____

_____ .

Something interesting about my native country is _____

_____ .

What I miss most about my native country is _____

_____ .

A problem my native country has is _____ .

I am proud of my native country because _____ .

The form of government in my native country is _____ .

People from my native country are <u>more/less</u> friendly than people in this country.

I think it is <u>easier/more difficult</u> to live in my native country than in this country.

One thing that is better in my native country than in this country is _____ .

One thing that is better in this country than in my native country is _____ .

If you want to visit my native country, the most important piece of advice I can give you is

_____ .

NOTES

Topic _____ Name _____ Date _____

My Family

My parents' names are/were _____.

I have/had _____ brothers and _____ sisters.

My marital status is _____.

I have/don't have children, _____ sons and _____ daughters.

My husband's/wife's name is _____.

My child's/children's name(s) is/are _____.

My child's/children's age(s) is/are _____.

My child/children live(s) in _____.

I have _____ grandchildren, _____ grandsons and _____ granddaughters.

Most of my family lives in _____.

Something my family enjoys doing together is _____

_____.

What makes me especially proud of my family is _____

_____.

NOTES

Topic _____ Name _____ Date _____

HOME SWEET HOME

In my native country, I lived in a/an _____.

Now, I am living in a/an _____.

My home in my native country had _____ rooms.

Now, my home has _____ rooms.

What I liked about my home in my native country was _____

_____.

What I like about my home in this country is _____

_____.

We paid about _____ ($) each month for housing in my native country.

Now, we pay about _____ ($) each month for housing.

The rent in my native country included these utilities: _____

_____.

The rent here includes these utilities: _____

_____.

If I could change one thing about my home in this country, I would _____

_____.

If I had enough money, I would/wouldn't move to another house or apartment because

_____.

NOTES

Topic _____ Name _____ Date _____

Election Day and Government

I <u>am/am not</u> a citizen of this country.

I <u>have/have never</u> voted before.

Some elected offices in my native country are _____

_____.

There are _____ major political parties in my native country.

We have elections: When? _____.

    How often? _____.

I think the best government should be _____

_____.

The most important job for the government is to

_____.

The biggest difference between the government here

and the government in my native country is

_____.

I <u>would/would not</u> like to work in the government because

_____.

One strength of the government in this country is

_____.

One weakness of the government in this country is

_____.

NOTES

Topic _____ Name _____ Date _____

Hobbies

Something I enjoy doing in my free time is …

_____.

I usually spend _____ minutes a week enjoying my hobby.

I usually spend _____ dollars on my hobby each month.

One benefit I get from my hobby is _____.

I've been enjoying my hobby for _____ years.

I learned my hobby from/by _____.

A hobby I used to enjoy when I was younger was _____.

The time of day when I usually do my hobby is _____

   because _____.

My friends/family/spouse feel(s) my hobby is _____.

If money and time were no problem, this is what I would do for my hobby.

_____

_____.

NOTES

Topic _____ Name _____ Date _____

Pets

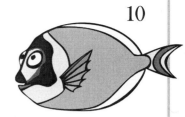

In my opinion, having a pet is _____ because _____
_____.

Dogs make <u>good/bad</u> pets because _____
_____.

Cats make <u>good/bad</u> pets because _____
_____.

Pets are good for children because _____
_____.

A good pet for someone who lives in an apartment is _____

   because _____.

Pets can be a problem when _____
_____.

When I was younger, I had a pet _____.

   Its name was _____.

In my native country, many people have pet _____.

Something that pet owners do or don't do which annoys me is

   _____.

The best thing about having a pet is _____ and the worst

   thing about having a pet is _____.

NOTES

Topic _____ Name _____ Date _____

MUSIC

THE INTERNATIONAL LANGUAGE

My favorite kind of music is _____.

My favorite musical artist is _____.

My favorite composer is _____.

I <u>like/don't like</u> to sing because _____.

I <u>can/cannot</u> play a musical instrument.

If I could learn to play (<u>a/another</u>) musical instrument, I would like to learn to play

the _____ because_____.

I <u>like/don't like</u> watching a ballet.

I <u>like/don't like</u> watching an opera.

I <u>like/don't like</u> American popular music because _____

_____.

I spend _____ minutes listening to music on the radio every day.

I <u>sing/don't sing</u> in the bathtub or shower.

I <u>can/cannot</u> sing a lullaby in my native language.

I <u>can/can't</u> dance well.

Music is an international language because _____

_____

_____.

NOTES

Topic _____ Name _____ Date _____

Transportation

My favorite way to travel is by _____ because

_____.

When I worked or went to school in my native country, I

traveled by _____.

Public transportation in this city is _____ because

_____.

Public transportation in my native country is _____

_____.

Traveling by airplane is _____.

In my native country, I could/couldn't drive a car.

In my native country, I could/couldn't ride a bicycle.

In my opinion, long car trips are _____ because

_____.

I think traveling by rocket ship would be _____

because _____.

If I could have a free ticket to anywhere in the world, I'd go

to _____ by _____.

NOTES

Topic _____ Name _____ Date _____

Grocery Shopping

I <u>enjoy/don't enjoy</u> grocery shopping because_____.

When I shop at a supermarket, I go to _____ (name)

  because_____.

I <u>use/don't use</u> coupons to save money.

I <u>read/don't read</u> the advertising circulars to see what's on sale before I begin shopping.

I <u>read/don't read</u> the nutrition labels on cans and boxes.

I <u>check/don't check</u> the unit pricing.

I <u>check/don't check</u> the expiration date on food I buy.

I go shopping _____. (how often?)

I usually buy these fruits and vegetables (produce): _____

_____.

I <u>buy/don't buy</u> my bread at a bakery.

I <u>buy/don't buy</u> my meat at a butcher shop.

I <u>buy/don't buy</u> <u>some/any</u> food items at an ethnic foods store.

I <u>check/don't check</u> my register receipt for errors.

I <u>make/don't make</u> a shopping list before I go to the store.

The first time I went to a supermarket in this country, I felt _____ because

_____.

NOTES

Topic _____ Name _____ Date _____

Celebrations

When I was a child in my native country, my favorite holiday was _____

_____.

A special way we celebrated this holiday was _____

_____.

We celebrate birthdays in my native country by _____

_____.

In my native country, New Year's Day was celebrated on _____(date) by

_____.

The biggest difference between wedding celebrations in my native country and

those in this country is _____.

In my native country, we exchange gifts at these holidays: _____

_____.

The biggest holiday of the calendar year in my native country is _____

_____.

Of all the holidays in this country, I most enjoy _____ because

_____.

I least enjoy (which holiday?) _____.

I'd like to have a holiday to celebrate _____

_____.

NOTES

Topic _____ Name _____ Date _____

Gifts

In my native country, gifts are given for these occasions: _____

_____.

Money <u>is/isn't</u> a good gift because _____.

When someone gives me a gift that I don't like, I usually _____

_____.

I think that handmade gifts are _____ because _____

_____.

The price of a gift <u>is/isn't</u> important because _____

_____.

Gift buying is sometimes difficult because _____

_____.

When I must buy a gift and I don't have any idea what to buy, I _____

_____.

When I am invited to a wedding, I usually give the bride and groom _____

_____.

When I was younger, a special gift I received from my parents was _____

_____.

The best gift I have ever received was _____ which was given to me by

_____ for _____ (occasion).

NOTES

Topic _____ Name _____ Date _____

Winter

In my native country, winter begins in the month of _____ and

finishes in the month of _____.

Winter weather in my native country is _____.

Winters in my native city are _____ than winters in my new city.

When I was younger, I used to enjoy _____ in the winter.

Before I came to this country, I <u>had/had never</u> seen snow.

Something I enjoy doing here in the winter is _____.

Something I don't enjoy doing here in the winter is _____.

The best thing about winter is _____.

The worst thing about winter is _____.

NOTES

Topic _____ Name _____ Date _____

Famous People

A famous person from my country is/was _____ who is/was

  famous for _____.

If I could meet one famous person, I'd like to meet _____ who is famous

  for their _____.

The qualities I most admire in this famous person is their _____

  _____.

I would/wouldn't like to be famous because _____

  _____.

The benefits of being famous are _____.

Some problems for famous people are _____.

An example of someone who is/was famous for positive reasons is /was _____

  _____.

An example of someone who is/was famous for negative reasons is/was _____

  _____.

If I could meet a famous person who is no longer alive, I'd like to meet _____

  because _____.

In my conversation with this person, I'd ask them about _____

  _____.

NOTES

Topic _____ Name _____ Date _____

Friendship

18

When I was younger, my best friend was _____.

We were friends for _____ years.

When we were together, we enjoyed _____.

Our friendship was important to us because _____

_____.

Today, my best friend is _____.

We have been friends for _____.

When we are together, we enjoy _____.

My best friend is special to me because _____

_____.

Making new friends in a new country is _____ because

_____.

The nicest thing a friend ever did for me was _____

_____.

The nicest thing I ever did for a friend was _____

_____.

Friends are important because _____

_____.

Friends are <u>more/less</u> important than family because _____

_____.

Copyright © 2003 Deborah F. Hitsky • **SURVEYS FOR CONVERSATION: WINTER** • 35

NOTES

Topic _____ Name _____ Date _____

Love

Love is . . .

_____ .

I <u>do/don't</u> believe in love at first sight. _____

_____ .

Some of the people I love are _____

_____ .

Some of the things I love are _____

_____ .

"Love makes the world go 'round" because _____

_____ .

I think romantic love is _____

_____ .

I <u>think/don't think</u> pre–marital sex is a good thing because _____

_____ .

Valentine's Day is _____

_____ .

"Love is blind" because _____

_____ .

You know you're in love when _____

_____ .

A _____ *'s love is the greatest love of all because* _____

_____ .

NOTES

Topic _____ Name _____ Date _____

Clothes

The color I look best in is _____.

I am most comfortable when I am wearing _____.

When I was a young student in my native country, I wore _____ to

school every day.

The store in this city where I buy most of my clothes is _____.

I like to shop at this store because it is _____

_____.

Clothing prices here are _____ than clothing prices in my native country.

I _follow/don't follow_ current clothing fads.

I _check/don't check_ the fabric care label in clothes.

My favorite material for summer clothing is _____ because

_____.

I _enjoy/don't enjoy_ shopping for clothing.

NOTES

Topic _____ Name _____ Date _____

Learning English

I started studying English in _____ (country) in _____(year).

The first time I came to school to study English, I felt _____ because

_____.

English is difficult because _____.

The most difficult thing about learning English is _____.

I wish I could _____ better English than I can now.

I spend _____ hours every day learning English.

I <u>do/do not</u> speak English outside of school.

I <u>do/do not</u> read or write English outside of school.

In my daily life, I have the biggest problem communicating in English when

_____.

I think learning a second language is easiest when you are _____ years old

   because _____.

The best advice I can give someone who is going to study English is _____

_____.

When I came here, I knew _____English.

When I compare my English now with my English when I first arrived here, I

   feel _____ because _____.

NOTES

Topic _____ Name _____ Date _____

Television

We got our first television in _____ (year).

I watch about _____ hours of TV each day.

My favorite television program is _____.

The time of the day when I enjoy watching TV is _____.

What I like about TV here is _____.

What I don't like about TV in this country is _____.

Television in my native country is _____ than TV here because

_____.

I think watching TV programs **helps/doesn't help** me learn English.

In my opinion, television is good because _____

_____.

I believe television is bad because _____

_____.

Television commercials **influence/don't influence** me when I shop because

_____.

Television **is/isn't** responsible for the increase in violence in this country.

The government **should/shouldn't** censor television programs.

NOTES

Topic _____ Name _____ Date _____

Work

When I was a child, I wanted to be a _____ when I grew up.

In my native country, I worked as a _____.

I started working when I was _____ years old.

The kind of education/training I had to have to prepare for my

   job was _____.

In my country, a worker doing my job works from _____(time)

   to _____(time) _____(how many?) days a week.

People doing my job in my native country earn about $_____

   a year.

Workers doing my job in my native country usually get _____

   vacation days a year.

In my native country, workers usually get these benefits:

_____.

What I liked about my job was _____.

What I didn't like about my job was _____.

I have had _____ (how many?) different jobs since I

   started working.

I think that the biggest problem for immigrants looking for jobs

   in this country is _____.

Improving my English will allow me to get a job as _____

_____.

NOTES

Topic _____ Name _____ Date _____

To Your Health

One thing I do for my health every day is _____.

I visit my doctor _____ times a year.

I visit the dentist _____ times a year.

I get _____ hours of sleep each night.

I exercise _____ times a week.

I eat _____ servings of fruits and vegetables each day.

I drink _____ glasses of water every day.

My blood pressure is <u>high/low</u> and my blood cholesterol is <u>high/low</u>.

In my opinion, medical care in this country is _____ because

_____.

Medical care in my native country is _____ because

_____.

A good health habit I have is _____.

A bad health habit I have is _____.

I could improve my health by _____.

Good health is important because _____.

NOTES

Topic _____ Name _____ Date _____

Spring Has Sprung!

In my native country:

Spring begins when _____.

The average spring temperature is _____.

Some spring holidays are _____.

Spring lasts for _____ months.

If you plan to visit my native country in the spring, be sure to wear _____

_____.

In this country:

An activity I do indoors in the spring is _____.

An activity I do outdoors in the spring is _____.

Spring makes me feel _____ because _____.

Spring is the best season for _____.

Spring is the worst season for _____.

If I rated the seasons 1 to 4, with 1 being my favorite, spring would be number _____.

NOTES

Topic _____ Name _____ Date _____

Exercise

When I lived in my native country, I walked <u>more/less</u> than I do today in this country.

When I was a child in my native country, I did this for exercise: _____

_____.

Today, I exercise about _____ times a week.

The kind of exercise I do now is _____.

The benefit I get from exercising is _____.

A problem I have that limits how much time I can exercise is _____

_____.

I prefer exercising <u>alone/with other people</u>.

After I exercise, I feel _____.

I think that people in my native country are in <u>better/worse</u> physical condition than

people in this country.

If I had more money or time, the kind of exercise I'd like to do is _____.

I would rather _____ than exercise.

NOTES

Topic _____ Name _____ Date _____

SPORTS

THE SPORTS I ENJOY AS A SPECTATOR ARE _____
_____.

THE SPORTS I ENJOY AS A PARTICIPANT ARE _____
_____.

THE SPORT I LIKE BEST IS _____ BECAUSE_____
_____.

THE SPORT I LIKE LEAST IS _____ BECAUSE _____
_____.

IN MY NATIVE COUNTRY, THE MOST POPULAR SPORTS ARE _____
_____.

SPORTS ARE GOOD BECAUSE _____
_____.

CHILDREN SHOULD TAKE PART IN SPORTS BECAUSE _____
_____.

PROFESSIONAL ATHLETES <u>ARE/AREN'T</u> PAID TOO MUCH.

PROFESSIONAL ATHLETES <u>ARE/AREN'T</u> IMPORTANT AS ROLE-MODELS
FOR YOUNG PEOPLE.

I'D RATHER _____THAN WATCH OR PARTICIPATE IN SPORTS.

NOTES

Topic _____ Name _____ Date _____

Food

What do people eat for breakfast in your native country?

_____

How many meals do people in your native country usually eat in a day?

_____

What time do people in your native country normally eat their meals?

_____

What do you like about the food in this country?

_____

What don't you like about the food here?

_____

Whose diet do you think is healthier, that of the people in your native country or that of the

people here ? _____ Why?

_____

What is a snack food that you enjoy eating? _____

What is a food that you can't buy in this city which you used to enjoy in your native country?

_____

Do you worry about preservatives in foods? _____

Are you a vegetarian? _____

What's your favorite food? _____

Do you "Eat to live or live to eat"? _____

NOTES

Topic _____ Name _____ Date _____

Living Here

I came to this country in _____(year) from _____ (country).

The reason I came here is _____.

I came here with a _____(type) visa.

I waited _____ years to come here.

I am planning to live in this country _____ (How long?)

The best thing about living here is _____.

The worst thing about living here is _____.

The greatest thing about this country is _____.

The worst thing about this country is _____.

When I compare the people here with the people in my native country, I think

    that _____.

I am homesick for _____ in my native country.

I don't miss the _____ in my native country.

NOTES

Topic _____ Name _____ Date _____

SAVE THE EARTH

Some evidence I've seen of pollution in my community is _____

_____.

Something I am personally doing to protect the environment is _____

_____.

Some things that cause environmental problems in this country are _____

_____.

Compared to this country, my native country has <u>many/few</u>

    environmental problems.

The government should _____ to preserve the

    environment.

An easy way people can improve their environment is to _____

_____.

The most wasteful thing I've seen people do is _____

_____.

In the future, cars will _____.

Recycling is_____.

Notes

Topic _____ Name _____ Date _____

Parents and Children

In my country:

The average family size is _____.

Mothers have these responsibilities in raising children: _____

_____.

Fathers have these responsibilities in raising children: _____

_____.

In this country:

Children are _____ compared with children in my native country.

Raising children is _____ than raising children in my native country.

Raising children today is more difficult than 100 years ago because _____

_____.

The ideal size of a family is _____.

The ideal age-spacing between children in a family is _____ years.

The biggest challenge in raising children is _____

_____.

When children grow up, their responsibility to their parents is _____

_____.

NOTES

Topic _____ Name _____ Date _____

My Mother

My mother's name is/was _____.

She was born in _____ (country or city) on _____ (date).

When she finished school, she became a _____.

She was _____ years old when I was born.

My mother has/had _____ children.

My mother has/had a special talent for _____.

I take after my mother in this way: _____.

I look like/don't look like my mother.

One important thing my mother teaches/taught me is/was _____

_____.

My mother helps/helped me _____.

She always encourages/encouraged me to _____

_____.

My mother likes/liked to _____.

When I do/did something good in school or at home, my mother rewards/rewarded

me by _____.

When I do/did something bad in school or at home, my mother punishes/punished

me by _____.

NOTES

Topic _____ Name _____ Date _____

The Computer Age

33

I <u>own/don't own</u> a computer, and I <u>am/am not</u> computer literate.

I use a computer to _____.

I spend _____minutes a day using the Internet.

In my opinion, the Internet is good because _____

_____.

A problem I see with the Internet is _____

_____.

The Internet <u>should/shouldn't</u> be regulated because _____

_____.

The computer hardware I'd like to own is _____.

The computer software I'd like to own is _____.

I think shopping on the Internet is _____ because

_____.

Studying English with the computer and/or the Internet is _____

because _____.

The biggest change computers and the Internet have made in our

lives is _____.

NOTES

Topic _____ Name _____ Date _____

34

INSTANT WIN!
LOTTERY
$10,000.00

If I won the Lottery

The first thing I'd do is _____.

I'd feel _____.

I would buy _____.

I would take a trip to _____.

I would put _____% of my money in the stock market.

I would put _____% of my money in the bank.

I would give my parents/children _____

_____.

I would use all/some/most of my money to benefit _____

_____

_____.

My life would be better/worse because _____

_____

_____.

NOTES

Topic _____ Name _____ Date _____

Our W🌐rld

35

The most serious problems in the world are _____

_____.

The three most important <u>inventions/discoveries</u> in the history of the world were

the _____

because _____.

The most important person in the history of the world was _____

because _____.

The most important event of the 20th century was _____

_____.

The country I admire most is _____.

We could solve a lot of world problems if people would _____

_____.

The dream of world peace is _____.

The most important lesson parents should teach their children for today's world

is to _____.

The United Nations is _____

_____.

The world will be a <u>better/worse</u> place 100 years from now because _____

_____.

NOTES

Topic _____ Name _____ Date _____

36

SPACE EXPLORATION

Space exploration <u>does/doesn't</u> interest me.

I <u>believe/don't believe</u> that there is life somewhere else in the universe.

The cost of space exploration <u>is/isn't</u> justified because _____

_____.

I <u>would/wouldn't</u> volunteer to be an astronaut because _____

_____.

The idea of myself traveling in space makes me feel _____.

People <u>should/shouldn't</u> be paying passengers on NASA space

explorations because _____.

The exploration of space has changed the world by _____

_____.

The exploration of space should be made by <u>governments/private industry</u>

because _____.

NOTES

Topic _____ Name _____ Date _____

37

My Father

My father's name _is/was_ _____.

He was born in _____ (city or country) in _____ (year).

His profession _is/was_ _____.

He met my mother in _____ (year).

They had _____ children.

I take after my father in this way: _____.

I _look like/don't look like_ my father.

My father _enjoys/enjoyed_ _____.

My father _is/was_ a good _____.

When my father _isn't/wasn't_ working, he _likes/liked_ to _____

_____.

My father _teaches/taught_ me to _____.

A father should be _____.

The role of a father today is different from that of a father many years ago because _____

_____

_____

NOTES

Topic _____ Name _____ Date _____

Weddings and Marriage

38

In your country:

Where do most couples get married?

_____

About how old are the men when they get married? _____

How old are the women? _____

Are marriages ever arranged by parents? _____

How do the bride and groom dress for their wedding? _____

_____

Who pays for the wedding? _____

What are typical gifts given to the bride and groom? _____

Do the bride and groom both wear wedding bands? _____

    On which finger of which hand? _____

Does the bride usually take her husband's family name? _____

Does the newly-married couple take a honeymoon? _____

Are there any superstitions related to weddings? _____

    If so, what are they? _____

Does the couple live apart from their families or with them? _____

How common is divorce in your native country? _____

Describe a typical traditional wedding. _____

_____

NOTES

Topic _____ Name _____ Date _____

39

Advice
for the Bride and Groom

For the bride: Be a good wife by _____.

For the groom: Be a good husband by _____.

What you must remember about marriage is that _____
_____.

Always be _____ to your spouse.

Never _____.

If you have a fight with your spouse, _____
_____.

Every day, don't forget to _____.

Make your life together special by _____.

Sometimes, do nice things for your spouse, like _____
_____.

Marriage is _____.

If you have children, _____
_____.

NOTES

Topic _____ Name _____ Date _____

40

Summer

The best season of all is _____.

In my native country the summer weather is _____.

What I like most about summer here is _____.

What I like least about summer here is _____.

When I compare summer in my native country with summer here, I _____

_____.

Last summer, the best thing I did was _____.

My favorite summer activity is_____.

For a summer vacation, I prefer <u>the seaside/a lake/the mountains</u>, or

_____.

This summer for fun <u>I'm/I'm not</u> going to _____.

This summer <u>I'm/I'm not</u> going to study _____.

• **SURVEYS FOR CONVERSATION: SUMMER** •

NOTES

Topic _____ Name _____ Date _____

IF

41

If I could be anyone in the world, I would be _____.

If I could be doing something else right now, I would be _____.

If I could be any age, I would be _____ years old.

If I could live anywhere in the world, I would choose to live in _____

because _____.

If I could have anything I wanted, I would ask for _____

because _____.

If I could change one thing about myself, I would change _____

_____.

If I could do one thing to change the world, I would _____

because _____.

If I could bring one person back to life, I would bring back _____.

If I could meet a famous person, I would like to meet _____.

If I could live in any time period (past, present, future), I'd want to live _____

because_____.

If I could learn how to do something new, I would learn how to

_____.

If I were rich, I would _____

_____

_____.

NOTES

Topic _____ Name _____ Date _____

In the Year 2100

42

People will be using _____ as transportation.

A cure will have been found for _____.

The drug war will _____.

Robots will be used for _____.

Television will have changed in this way:_____

_____.

Countries <u>will/will not</u> continue to have military forces and nuclear weapons.

Terrorism will be _____.

Schools will be different from today in this way: _____

_____.

The food people eat will be different in this way: _____

_____.

Life expectancy for men will be _____ and for women _____ years.

Marriage and the family unit will be different in this way: _____

_____.

Life will be <u>better/worse</u> than today because _____

_____.

NOTES

Topic _____ Name _____ Date _____

Birth and Death

43

The average married couple in my native country has _____ children.

Is there a special ceremony following a birth in your native country? _____

If "yes", describe it. _____

Is abortion permitted in your native country? _____ When, if ever, should it be permitted?

_____

_____

How should abortion be limited? _____

_____

The average life expectancy for women in my native country is _____ years; the average

    life expectancy for men is _____ years.

Is there a special ceremony following a death in your native country? _____

    If "yes", describe it. _____

Which is more common in your native country, burial or cremation? _____

Do you believe in an afterlife? _____ heaven? _____ hell? _____

    reincarnation? _____

How do you feel about euthanasia? _____

How do you feel about suicide? _____

NOTES

Topic _____ Name _____ Date _____

44

War and Peace

War <u>is/is not</u> inevitable.

If World War III ever happened, the result would be _____

_____.

In times of war, people become more _____.

A war that my native country participated in was fought against

_____(country) in _____(year).

In my life, my experience with war has been _____

_____.

Should children play with war toys? _____   Why or why not?

_____.

The United Nations <u>is/is not</u> helping to achieve world peace.

The United States, as the world's strongest country, must

_____ to keep peace.

Maintaining a strong military <u>does/does not</u> prevent wars.

World peace will be possible when people _____

_____.

NOTES

Topic _____ Name _____ Date _____

Crime

45

Do you think crime is a bigger problem in your native country or in this country?

_____

Is the death penalty used in your native country? _____

Do you agree or disagree with capital punishment? _____ Why?

_____

In your opinion, how can crime be reduced? _____

What should be the punishment for first-degree murder? _____

In your opinion, what can be done about illegal drug dealers and drug users?

_____

What do you think is the youngest age a person should be tried as an adult?

_____ Why? _____

Have you ever been a victim of crime? _____

If yes, explain. _____

Do you worry about crime? _____ What kind? _____

_____

Is money "the root of all evil"? _____ Why or why not? _____

_____

NOTES

Topic _____ Name _____ Date _____

46

Books

I first learned to read when I was _____ . (age)

I was taught to read by my _____.

Now, I read _____ . (how often?)

My favorite time of the day for reading is _____ because _____

_____.

I read/don't read newspapers in English because _____

_____.

My favorite kinds of books are _____.

I read/don't read English magazines because _____

_____.

I think people today are reading more/less than they did many years ago

   because _____.

In my native country, the government does/doesn't control the publishing

   of books, magazines, and newspapers.

Censorship by the government is never/sometimes a good idea because

_____.

The best book I ever read was _____.

This book was about _____

_____.

NOTES

Topic _____ Name _____ Date _____

47

School Days

I started going to school when I was _____ years old.

Most of my classes in elementary school had about _____ students.

My favorite subject in elementary school was _____.

In my native country, I had about _____ minutes of homework each night.

In my native country, I attended school from _____ o'clock to _____ o'clock,

_____ days a week.

The schools I attended had about _____ (how many?) students.

My favorite teacher was _____ (name) who taught me

_____.

The reason I liked this teacher was _____.

The most difficult class I ever studied was _____.

One thing I didn't like about school in my native country was _____

_____.

When I went to school in my native country, students who didn't behave

themselves in class were punished by _____.

When I compare my school in my native country with school in this country,

I think _____.

NOTES

Topic _____ Name _____ Date _____

On Vacation

48

What I like about traveling is _____.

What I don't like about traveling is _____.

If I could afford it, I'd like to travel to _____.

The greatest trip I've ever taken was to _____.

Number these in order of your preference: 1-5 (1 is the best): sea cruise _____

   bus trip _____ camping _____ lake cottage _____ mountain hiking _____

When I pack for a trip, I tend to take <u>more/less</u> clothing than I use.

The best souvenir I ever brought back from a trip was a _____

_____.

I <u>like/don't like</u> taking organized tours.

This is what I would do on my next vacation: _____

_____.

NOTES

Topic _____ Name _____ Date _____

USEFUL EXPRESSIONS

As I was saying . . .

As for me . . .

Do I understand you to say . . .?

Could you clarify . . .?

Could you please . . .?

Do you agree (that) . . . ?

Did you say . . . ?

Excuse me, but . . .

From my point of view . . .

Here's another idea.

How can you say . . .?

I (don't) agree with . . .

I disagree with . . .

I beg to differ with you, but . . .

I beg your pardon?

I (don't) believe . . .

I can't/don't understand how . . .

I hate to contradict you, but . . .

I'm not sure, but I . . .

I side with _____

I think that . . .

I (don't) understand why . . .

I would prefer . . .

I would rather . . .

If I understand you . . .

If I were . . .

If . . . then . . .

In my own experience, . . .

In my opinion, . . .

It is my opinion that . . .

In your shoes, I would . . .

Let me explain how I feel.

Looking at it another way . . .

My feeling is . . .

My own opinion is . . .

My point of view is . . .

Not everyone will agree with me, but . . .

On the other hand . . .

Please defend your answer.

Please explain . . .

Please repeat what you said.

Please tell me . . .

Say what you will, but . . .

What do you mean?

What do you think of . . . ?

What I think is that . . .

What's important is . . .

What's your opinion of . . . ?

Why do you say . . .?

With all due respect, . . .

With respect to what you said . . .

Would you please . . .?

You're entitled to your opinion, but . . .

You said that . . .

NOTES

Topic _____ Name _____ Date _____

TEACHER'S GUIDE

The purpose of *Surveys for Conversation* is to stimulate effective conversation practice. The surveys are used over two days. On day one, the conversation topic is introduced, and the survey worksheets are assigned for homework. On the following day, the completed surveys are the basis for conducting a conversation.

By doing the surveys as homework, the students have a chance to think about their ideas, look up the words they need to express them, and have a written copy to bring back to class for sharing. Because they've prepared their responses and had an opportunity to think about the topic before the actual discussion, the student anxiety level is lowered, and the resulting conversation is more focused, effective, relaxed, and enjoyable.

Virtually all of the surveys can be used at any proficiency level, from high beginner to advanced. The survey topics are suited to a range of age and interest levels. Use or adapt the surveys in a way that is appropriate for your class.

There is a blank "Notes" page on the backside of each survey. This page can be used as a journal, in which the students record their thoughts **after** the conversation. The page can also be used simply to note words, phrases, information or questions that may occur **during** the conversation. The entire page, front and back, is detachable, and can be removed and handed in.

The 48 surveys are arranged to follow the seasons of a school year, 12 topics for each season, beginning with the fall. Each season's surveys include some of the typical activities of that season. Thus, the completed surveys and the notes page can serve as a personal record of an academic year's progress. However, the surveys can also be used in any order, and there is no requirement that every survey must be completed. In fact, the surveys can be used quite effectively in virtually any kind of program at any time of the year.

There is also another kind of progression to the topics. The earlier topics focus on personal information, while the later topics focus on issues. Along with this topical progression, there will also be an increase in the lexical and grammatical challenge that the students will encounter as they discuss their personal opinions and contemporary issues.

In addition to stimulating conversation, the surveys and ensuing conversation can also help to expand the students' vocabulary. On pages 102-105, there is a list of words that may be unfamiliar to the students as they complete the surveys and carry out the conversations. It may be necessary to go over these **"lexical challenges."** (See Step 2 in the Teaching Procedure for Day One, page 101). Although it is impossible to predict with complete accuracy what words will be new to the students, these words are not at the 600-word level in Pro Lingua's *The Learner's Lexicon**.

The Extension Activities beginning on page 116 are suggested for following up on the conversations. The surveys can also be used to augment or supplement content-based units of study, to explore cultural aspects of North American English, and to exemplify specific grammar points. In short, this collection of 48 surveys offers considerable flexibility, and may be easily adapted to a variety of teaching situations.

----

* *The Learner's Lexicon* is a compilation of 2400 words that are important to the learner of English. The first 600 words are considered words that a learner at the high beginner level should know.

TEACHING PROCEDURE

The recommended **teaching procedure** is outlined below. However, as every teaching situation is different, it should be modified as the situation demands.

Day One

(1)   Introduce the topic. Describe it very generally, and/or ask the students to tell what they know about the topic.

(2)   Go over the vocabulary associated with the topic by going over the words you think they might need for understanding the survey questions and for carrying out a conversation. The list of **lexical challenges** beginning on page 102 can be used as a reference.

(3)   Have the students open their books to the survey and go over it for comprehension to be sure the students understand the questions.

(4)   Assign the the survey for homework.

Day Two

(1)   Have the students share their responses to the survey. This can be done in pairs, small groups, or as an entire class. In some cases the responses can be tallied, and the result used as an opinion poll.

(2)   The survey sharing can then be followed by a discussion of the topic.

The **extension activities** beginning on page 106 include suggestions on how to follow up and extend the conversation topic.

On page 97 there is a list of **useful expressions** that are commonly used in discussions and conversations. They can be introduced a few at a time at the beginning of each conversation session. They can also be written on the board for on-going reference and use, or they can be written on index cards and handed out to the students. Each student can be given the same card, for example, "In my opinion. . ." or they can each be given a different card to use at least once during the course of the conversation. The list of useful expressions can be detached and used in each of the conversations.

LEXICAL CHALLENGES

LEXICAL CHALLENGES

14 Celebrations · *page 27*

special
to celebrate
a birthday
a wedding
to exchange
a gift
a calendar year

15 Gifts · *page 29*

an occasion
handmade
a bride
a groom
to receive

16 Winter · *page 31*

snow

17 Famous People · *page 33*

famous
a quality
to admire
a reason
positive
negative
dead
a conversation

18 Friendship · *page 35*

together
friendship

19 Love · *page 37*

at first sight
'round
romantic
pre-marital sex
blind

20 Clothes · *page 39*

comfortable
to wear
current
a fad
fabric
a label
material

21 Learning English · *page 41*

daily
to communicate

22 Television · *page 43*

a commercial
to influence
responsible
to increase
violence
a censor

23 Work · *page 45*

to grow up
years old
education
training
to prepare
to earn
immigrant
to allow

24 Health · *page 47*

health
a dentist
to exercise
a serving
blood pressure
cholesterol
medical
a habit

SPRING

25 Spring · *page 49*

average
to last
to plan
indoors
outdoors
to rate

26 Exercise · *page 51*

to limit
to prefer
physical condition
would rather

27 Sports · *page 53*

a spectator
a participant
to take part in
professional
an athlete
a role-model

LEXICAL CHALLENGES

28 Food • *page 55*

a meal
normally
a diet
a snack
a preservative

29 Living Here • *page 57*

a visa
homesick

30 Save the Earth • *page 59*

evidence
pollution
a community
personally
to protect
the environment
to cause
to preserve
wasteful
recycling

31 Parents & Children • *page 61*

to raise
ideal
age-spacing
a challenge

32 Mother • *page 63*

a talent
to encourage
to reward
to punish
to take after
to look like

33 Computer Age • *page 65*

to regulate
hardware
software
literate

34 Lottery • *page 67*

to win
a lottery
% (percent)
the stock market

35 Our World • *page 69*

serious
an invention
a discovery
history
to solve
a dream
peace

36 Space Exploration • *page 71*

space
exploration
the universe
to justify
a volunteer
an astronaut
a passenger
private industry

Summer

37 Father • *page 73*

profession
role

38 Weddings • *page 75*

a couple
to dress
typical
a wedding band
a honeymoon
apart
common
divorce
traditional
to arrange
a superstition

39 Advice • *page 77*

spouse

40 Summer • *page 79*

the seaside
a lake
a mountain
fun

41 If • *page 81*

to bring back
a time period
past
present
future
rich

LEXICAL CHALLENGES

42 2100 • *page 83*

a cure
the drug war
a robot
military force
a nuclear weapon
the life expectancy
a family unit

43 Birth and Death • *page 85*

a ceremony
a birth
to follow
an abortion
to permit
to limit
death
burial
cremation
afterlife
heaven
hell
reincarnation
euthanasia
suicide

44 War and Peace • *page 87*

war
inevitable
a result
a role
to participate
to fight
against
an experience
a goal
to achieve
a toy
an organization
to maintain
to prevent

45 Crime • *page 89*

crime
punishment
first-degree murder
to try
an adult
the death penalty
to disagree
illegal
a victim
capital punishment
to reduce
the root
evil

46 Books • *page 91*

a magazine
to control
to publish

47 School Days • *page 93*

an elementary school
a subject
homework
to attend
to behave

48 On Vacation • *page 95*

to afford
a sea cruise
camping
a cottage
hiking
to pack
to tend to
a souvenir

EXTENSION ACTIVITIES

1 Let Me Introduce Myself - page 1

1. Tabulate the results of the survey: What's the most popular color, etc. Do it by male/female responses.

2. Create a "hot seat" and choose a student to sit in it while others ask them questions.

3. Invite the students to bring something (or someone) to school that is special to them and share with the class.

4. From time to time play "Who Am I?" Say, "I'm thinking of someone whose favorite food is ice cream." Choose students to be the leader.

5. Make a class address book and give a copy to each student. This can be useful later, when students are absent or ill. Create a chain for spreading information like school cancellations to the students.

2 Information Please - page 3

1. Role-play television talk-show interviews, having the "host" ask the "guest" some of the survey questions, and/or other questions. Let the "audience" ask questions, too.

2. Play this chain game: The first student begins, "I enjoy _____." The next student says, "_____enjoys _____, and I enjoy _____. The third student will have to announce what the first two students enjoy doing, and then add their own favorite activity, etc.

3. Have volunteers pantomime their answers to question 10 (Something I can do very well.) Let the class guess what the activity is.

3 Back to School - page 5

1. Make a copy of each student's survey. Review it occasionally during the year. At the end of the course, pass them back and discuss them. Were the goals realistic? Which goals were realized? Which goals were not met? Why?

2. Appoint a field trip committee to research and plan excursions.

3. Ask the students to keep a notebook with weekly entries of new vocabulary they have learned.

EXTENSION ACTIVITIES

4 Fall - page 7

1. If you live in an area where the leaves change color, collect leaves from different trees and learn the names of the trees.

2. Do some lessons on the fall holidays.

3. Have the students share fall celebrations from their countries.

4. Collect recipes for apple pie, pumpkin pie, cranberry sauce, roast turkey, etc., and, if possible, prepare one or more.

5. Have a Thanksgiving feast. Read recipes, plan a menu, appoint shoppers, assign cooks, set the table.

5 My Native Country - page 9

1. In a multicultural class do oral or written "Native Country" reports.

2. Encourage the students to bring in art, photos, clothing, food, etc. from their native countries.

3. Put up a world map. Stick pins in each of the students' countries and put the students' photos near the pins.

4. Stage an ethnic fair. Invite other classes to enjoy music, crafts, food, photographs, videos, costumes, etc.

6 My Family - page 11

1. Encourage the students to bring family photograph albums to share.

2. Have the students make family trees and talk about them.

3. In a future conversation class compare families in this country with families "back home."

4. Create a list of family relationships: *in-laws, niece, nephew,* etc. Also include marital status terms: *single, separated, divorced, widowed,* etc.

EXTENSION ACTIVITIES

7 Home Sweet Home - page 13

1. Invite the students to bring in photographs of their native country homes.

2. Have the students do scale floor plans of their homes and then show and tell in pairs.

3. Do this survey in correlation with a unit on housing, including real estate ads, leases, abbreviations, etc.

8 Election Day - page 15

1. This survey, assigned near an Election Day, can be a springboard for a study of local and national politics, culminated by a mock election, complete with candidates, campaigns, exit polls, speeches, etc.

2. In a national election, particularly a presidential election, tape the debates/ speeches for listening practice and comprehension.

3. Use the survey in conjunction with a study of the national constitution.

4. Visit a polling place on Election Day. Call the city clerk for a sample ballot.

9 Hobbies - page 17

1. Invite the students to share their hobbies by bringing their work to school. Some interesting demonstrations could follow, like Chinese paper cutting or Hmong embroidery, for example.

2. Have a craft fair, allowing the students to display and describe their work.

3. Visit an art fair or craft fair and encourage the students to ask the vendors about their work.

4. Identify any collectors in the class. Invite them to display or describe their collections.

EXTENSION ACTIVITIES

10 Pets - page 19

1. Have the pet owners share photos of their pets.

2. Visit an animal shelter or a pet shop.

3. Invite a veterinarian or shelter worker to come to class and talk about pet ownership in this country.

4. Watch an animal movie, like *Old Yeller, My Dog Skip,* or *Lassie.*

5. Tape and watch a segment of the TV channel, *Animal Planet.*

6. Collect a number of animal idioms, such as "raining cats and dogs," "eats like a bird," "fish out of water," etc.

7. Match adjectives with animals: *wise owl, sly fox, proud peacock,* etc.

11 Music, The International Language - page 21

1. Ask students who play an instrument to bring it to class and play and talk about it.

2. Introduce and learn the lyrics to a folk song, a popular song or a patriotic song.

3. In the appropriate season, play a movement from Vivaldi's "Four Seasons" and have the students write their thoughts as they listen. This can be coordinated with the seasonal progression of the surveys.

12 Transportation - page 23

1. Have the students work with a road or street map and give directions from one place to another.

2. Photocopy a train, bus, or plane schedule and practice reading it.

3. Role-play buying a ticket at a terminal or over the phone.

4. Have the students create the sequence of steps involved in using a subway or going through security at an airport.

5. Groups of students can plan vacations. This can include budgeting, mapping the route, researching and selecting hotels, choosing points of interest, etc.

EXTENSION ACTIVITIES

13 Grocery Shopping - page 25

1. Bring in and practice reading store coupons.

2. Bring in two circulars from different markets and compare prices.

3. Study a nutrition label and/or a nutrition chart.

4. Have the students work in pairs to make a shopping list. Take them to a grocery store and carry out an imaginary shopping trip by locating and writing down the aisle number and price for each item.

5. Teach "taste" adjectives. Bring in foods to illustrate *sour, spicy, hot, salty, sweet, bitter, creamy, chunky*, etc.

14 Celebrations - page 17

1. Make a calendar noting everyone's birthdays and native holidays.

2. Celebrate birthdays in class.

3. Assign various holidays for oral and/or written reports.

4. Learn songs and poetry that correlate with holidays.

5. Organize bulletin boards featuring holidays.

6. Produce pageants to celebrate national holidays. The students can read poetry, sing songs, perform skits, etc. Invite guests and take photos.

7. Celebrate some holidays from the students' native countries.

15 Gifts - page 29

1. Have a holiday gift exchange. Pick names and limit the cost of the gift. On the appointed day, have the students guess what's in their gift and who gave it.

2. Bring in an assortment of greeting cards. Explain and discuss the occasions and pass them around for reading practice.

3. Create greeting cards for an upcoming holiday.

4. Have one student demonstrate wrapping a package while others describe what they are doing.

5. Create greeting cards using a software program and send them to someone.

EXTENSION ACTIVITIES

16 Winter - page 31

1. Have the students explain the steps involved in doing a winter activity, for example, making a snowman, skiing, dressing warmly.

2. Have the students work with recipes for different kinds of soup.

3. Learn the names for winter clothing.

4. Have the students do reports on the winter holidays.

5. Have the students research winter sporting events. Give each student a different event to report on.

6. Do a project on the Winter Olympics.

7. Make a winter vocabulary list with words such as *sleet, ice, blizzard, slush*, etc.

17 Famous People - page 33

1. Play "Who Am I?" in which a student poses as a famous person and answers only yes/no questions from the other students. They try to guess who the famous person is in 10 questions.

2. Assign short speeches or written reports on famous people.

3. View some biographical movies such as *The Miracle Worker, Chaplin, Ali, A Beautiful Mind.* Follow up with reviews of the film.

4. Role-play interviews with famous people. Each student researches a famous person and then is interviewed by the others.

18 Friendship - page 35

1. Introduce the proverb, "A friend in need is a friend indeed," and ask the students to share proverbs from their own country about friendship.

2. Have the students write about their own best friends.

3. Play Simon and Garfunkle's song, "Bookends." Prepare the lyrics and then cut each line into a strip. Let groups of students reassemble them. You could also white out selected words from the entire script, have the students listen and fill in the missing words.

EXTENSION ACTIVITIES

19 Love - page 37

1. Read about Valentine's Day.

2. Make Valentine cards.

3. Choose a popular love song, listen to it, and learn the lyrics. Some suggestions: "Perhaps Love," (Pavarotti and John Denver), "Love is a Many-Splendored Thing," or "The Rose."

4. Collect "love" sayings: *All's fair in love and war. Love makes the world go 'round*, etc.

20 Clothes - page 39

1. Bring in clothing ads from newspapers or fashion magazines. Have pairs or small groups choose appropriate clothing for church, a football game, working in an office, etc.

2. Invite the students to bring in clothing items from their native countries.

3. Have a fashion show. Each student prepares a 3x5 card describing what they are wearing. An emcee reads the cards as the models parade by.

4. Go over the various clothing sizes (shirt, pants, shoes, hat, dress) and have the students determine their own sizes. You may need to bring in a tape measure.

5. Have a rummage sale. Invite the students to bring in good, used clothes, sort and size them, price them and then sell them for a class party or trip.

21 Learning English - page 41

1. Ask the students to brainstorm a list of situations where they must use English. Have them rate, on a scale of 1 to 5, how comfortable they are in these situations. This information can help you in planning later lessons.

2. Have the students look up and study dictionary entries to help them understand all of the information contained in each entry.

3. From time to time, carry out feedback and evaluation sessions to help the students track their progress in English.

4. Keep journals and encourage the students to write entries to describe their frustrations and triumphs.

Extension Activities

22 Television - page 43

1. Practice using a newspaper TV guide.

2. Hold a debate on the the idea that television violence is bad for children.

3. Produce a TV program, having students read the news, weather, and sports. Some students could prepare commercials.

4. Visit a television studio. If possible, arrange for the students to be part of the audience.

5. Discuss commercials. Talk about selling techniques and how they influence people. Discuss personal reactions to particular commercials. Tape a few and bring them in.

23 Work - page 45

1. Do a thematic unit on reading and responding to job ads, filling out applications, writing resumes, cover letters.

2. Practice job interviews.

3. Visit an employment agency or a job fair.

4. Ask the school counselor to give a presentation.

24 Health - page 47

1. Visit a hospital or other health agency.

2. Work on medical vocabulary, including the names for physician specialties (cardiologist, orthopedist, etc.).

3. Have the students keep a health journal, recording their daily habits (sleep, exercise, nutrition).

4. Practice filling out health information forms.

5. Invite a health care worker to speak to the class.

EXTENSION ACTIVITIES

25 Spring Has Sprung! - page 49

1. Study the spring holidays: St. Patrick's Day, Easter, Passover, Good Friday, Earth Day, Cinco de Mayo, Memorial Day, Mother's Day, May Day.

2. Do a unit on gardening. Learn the vocabulary of gardening. Read and study seed packets. Plant seeds in cups.

3. Take a walk around the area to identify flowers, shrubs and trees.

4. Teach the names of baby animals.

5. Bring in a seed catalog to learn the names of plants.

6. Read the labels on pesticides and fertilizers.

26 Exercise - page 51

1. Watch an exercise program on TV and follow along.

2. Visit a gym and learn about exercise equipment.

3. Learn how to take a person's pulse.

4. Have the students demonstrate the exercises they do.

27 Sports - page 53

1. Ask the students to prepare oral presentations of their favorite sports.

2. Learn the game of baseball: how it's played, its history, the names of players, etc., and, if possible, attend a game. Or, videotape an inning or two.

3. Do research on the biographies of sports figures and do written reports.

4. Ask the students to teach a game from their native country.

5. Learn the terms, rules, and procedures for bowling, and then take the class to a bowling alley.

EXTENSION ACTIVITIES

28 Food - page 55

1. Work on reading recipes.
2. Watch a segment of a TV food program.
3. Put up a nutrition chart and, from time to time, have the students check the nutritional value of a recent meal.
4. Do a role-play for eating at a restaurant.
5. Visit a farmers' market or farmstand.
6. Encourage the students to share their diets, especially if they follow special religious dietary laws.

29 Living Here - page 57

1. Create a class collection of personal immigration stories.
2. Read about famous immigrants.
3. Do a unit on the different groups of immigrants to North America: where they settled, what they contributed.
4. Invite older immigrants to come to class and tell their sories.
5. Show a video: for example, *Moscow on the Hudson*, *Green Card*, *or The Joy Luck Club*.
6. Discuss the immigrant services available to your students.

30 Save the Earth - page 59

1. Plan and carry out an Earth Day (April 22) program.
2. Prepare a bulletin board on environmental issues from the paper. Update it weekly with new stories.
3. Have the class do a project like making posters on recycling, littering, or conserving electricity.
4. "Adopt a street" and clean it regularly.
5. Organize a class clean-up of a park, river, or pond.

31 Parents and Children - page 61

1. Have the students collect and bring in newspaper cartoons depicting parents and children, for example, "For Better or Worse."
2. Research the community for child and family services. Find out where they are and what they do.
3. Visit a day-care center.
4. Invite a social worker to talk to the class on current trends in child-raising.
5. Do a unit on adoption, including cross-cultural adoptions.

32 My Mother - page 63

1. Write poems or messages about mothers for Mother's Day cards.
2. Have the students write a biography of their mother or grandmother.
3. Ask the students to share ideas on gifts for mothers.

33 The Computer Age - page 65

1. Create a computer vocabulary list.
2. Use newspaper ads to comparison shop for computer hardware and/or software.
3. If computers are available:
   — use search engines to find ESL websites and review them.
   — organize electronic "penpals" with other English language students.
   — have the students submit material to an ESL website, like the Internet TESL journal (http://iteslj.org/)

EXTENSION ACTIVITIES

34 If I Won the Lottery - page 67

1. Collect idioms about money and wealth, for example, "from rags to riches," "born with a silver spoon in his mouth,""All that glitters is not gold."

2. Discuss a lucky number for the class and buy a class lottery ticket.

3. Learn the lyrics of "If I were a Rich Man" from "Fiddler on the Roof," or "Money, Money, Money" by ABBA.

4. Hold a debate: Can money buy happiness?

5. Read and discuss the poem, "Richard Cory" by E.A.Robinson.

6. Discuss the ethics of state-run lotteries.

35 Our World - page 69

1. Do a weekly "News of the Week in Review" with each student reporting from different areas.

2. Each week review information from a different country.

3. Role-play an international meeting with the students being representatives from different countries. Have them circulate, meet, and share information.

4. Role-play a press conference with a world leader. Have "reporters" ask questions and write up the interview afterwards.

36 Space Exploration - page 71

1. Tape and show a segment of *Star Trek* or *Star Wars*.

2. Do a research project on the history of space exploration.

3. Hold a debate on the value of space exploration.

4. Watch for and follow the progress of the next space launch.

5. Search the web for sites on space exploration and download short segments.

6. Learn the names of the planets and/or the zodiacal constellations.

EXTENSION ACTIVITIES

37 My Father - page 73

1. Design Father's Day cards with written messages.

2. Have each student bring in an object or a picture of something that was important to their father and characterizes him. They explain it to the class.

3. Share ideas about gifts that are appropriate for fathers.

4. Have the students bring in an unlabeled photo of their father. Collect them and then see if the class can identify the fathers.

38 Weddings and Marriage - page 75

1. Bring in a video that shows a wedding (*Father of the Bride, The Graduate*).

2. Plan a wedding. First, establish the sequence of events leading up to the wedding.

3. Carry out a mock wedding with everyone taking a role: bride, groom, flower girl, parents, etc.

4. Read engagement and/or wedding announcements in the paper.

5. Married students can bring in various mementos to show and explain.

39 Advice for the Bride and Groom - page 77

1. Construct a list of household rules: who's responsible for what.

2. Role-play a marriage counselor giving advice to a couple who are not doing well.

3. Write and answer advice letters (such as "Dear Abby") about marriage problems.

40 Summer - page 79

1. Brainstorm all the events that take place only in the summer.

2. Have each student research and report on imaginary, ideal summer vacations.

3. Have the students write or tell about their best summer experience.

4. Have an end-of-the-year class picnic.

5. Compile a summer reading list.

EXTENSION ACTIVITIES

41 If - page 81

1. Listen to and learn the lyrics of John Lennon's "Imagine."

2. Read the poem "If" by Rudyard Kipling.

3. Discuss these proverbs and then have the students write an "if" proverb of their own.

   __ If "ifs" and "ands" were pots and pans, there'd be no work for tinker's hands.

   __ If wishes were horses, beggars would ride.

4. Watch the character Tevye sing "If I Were a Rich Man" from "Fiddler on the Roof." Make a list of the things Tevye would do if he were rich.

42 In the Year 2100 - page 83

1. Divide the class into groups and give each group a room in the house. Have each group develop a description of how this room would look in 2100.

2. Choose a local scene that everyone is familiar with. Show a picture of how it looks today. Then each group creates a picture of how it would look in 2100.

3. Have the class decide what to put in a time capsule to be opened in the year 2100.

43 Birth and Death - page 85

1. Research and report on the latest vital statistics.

2. From the Vital Records Office, get applications for birth and death certificates and practice filling out the forms.

3. Do a research project on the major religions and their attitudes toward burial practices, afterlife, abortion, euthanasia, and suicide.

4. Read some obituaries, and then write one (an imaginary person, or their own).

5. Create sympathy cards, new baby announcements, and congratulations cards.

EXTENSION ACTIVITIES

44 War and Peace - page 87

1. Have groups research and report on wars from the past.

2. Have groups research and report on current conflicts around the world.

3. Hold a mock United Nations session in which the members debate a current world conflict, for example, should the UN send observers or peacekeepers to _____?

4. Hold a debate on the pros and cons of pacifism.

5. Learn songs of war and protest. For example: "Where Have All the Flowers Gone?" "When Johnny Comes Marching Home."

45 Crime - page 89

1. Bring in news stories about crimes. Have small groups discuss and decide on appropriate punishments and then compare their decisions.

2. Invite a lawyer or police officer to speak to the class.

3. Create a sequence of events for dealing with a crime. For example: arrest, detention, arraignment, charge, and the trial and sentencing.

4. Conduct a mock trial.

5. Take a field trip to a court or police station.

6. Research and discuss an accused person's rights in this country.

46 Books - page 91

1. Schedule a trip to the school or community library.

2. Establish a regular "free reading" period.

3. Have each student bring in a different magazine and describe its contents.

4. Ask the students to create a reading plan for the summer.

5. Write book reviews.

6. Have a book swap or sale.

EXTENSION ACTIVITIES

47 School Days - page 93

1. Review the year's work with the students and have them write their own progress report.

2. Do a research project on current school issues, such as violence in schools.

3. Investigate the local school system and create a report on its organization, policies, personnel.

4. Attend a school board or PTA meeting. Take notes and discuss it afterward.

5. Compare grading systems in the students' countries and in this country.

48 On Vacation - page 95

1. Write letters to tourist bureaus requesting brochures.

2. Practice map reading with road maps.

3. Invite the students to bring in photos or souvenirs from previous vacations and talk about them.

4. If summer is approaching, have the students make a presentation on their real or imaginary summer vacations.

5. Bring in a travel video.

6. Show the video "European Vacation."

RESOURCES

Index Card Games for ESL. 7 games using index cards to learn vocabulary, practice grammar structures, and build confidence and competance in conversation. For each game there are photocopyable samples that are easy, moderate, and difficult.

More Index Card Games for English. 9 more games using index cards appropriate for students at different proficiency levels. These games stress speaking and listening skills. As in Index Card Games for ESL, though in a smaller format, all the sample material is photocopyable.

Match It! Another photocopyable collection of index card games. The game "Match It!" is similar to "Concentration." The materials range in difficulty from basic/easy to advanced/difficult.

Pronunciation Card Games. A photocopyable collection of index card games working on minimal pairs, syllabification, stress, and intonation.

The Great Big BINGO Book. A photocopyable collection of bingo games, providing practice with grammar, vocabulary, writing, pronunciation, and cultural information.

Shenanigames. 49 games practicing specific grammar points of graded difficulty. They are appropriate for students from middle school to adult.

The ESL Miscellany. A single-volume teacher resource book with dozens of lists of grammatical information, vocabulary topics, cultural information, miscellaneous material (punctuation rules, spelling rules, abbreviations, maps, gestures, etc.). A great resource for developing games and other lesson materials.

Lexicarry. Hundreds of uncaptioned pictures which get students talking about language, learning vocabulary, and discussing what language is appropriate in the pictured situations. Includes functions, sequences, operations, topics, and proverbs. Ideal for pair and small group work. A word list in the back allows for self-study. Wordlists in other languages and a teacher's guide are free at www.Lexicarry.com. Over 4500 words.

English Interplay: Surviving. A first text for beginning adolescents and adults. Students work in pairs, triads, and small groups, learning basic grammar, spelling, pronunciation, numbers, and a 700-word vocabulary that is necessary for survival in an English-speaking world.

Rhymes and Rhythms. 32 original poems/chants for practicing basic grammar and pronunciation and learning vocabulary. The rhymes progress from short and easy to longer and more challenging. This is a photocopyable text with an optional cassette recording of all the rhymes read once deliberately and then read again at natural speed.

Pro Lingua Associates • 800-366-4775 • www.ProLinguaAssociates.com